The
PRAYER
of JABEZ

BIBLE STUDY
FOR PERSONAL OR GROUP USE

BRUCE WILKINSON
with DAVID KOPP

Multnomah® Publishers *Sisters, Oregon*

THE PRAYER OF JABEZ BIBLE STUDY
published by Multnomah Publishers, Inc.

© 2001 by Exponential, Inc.
International Standard Book Number: 1-57673-979-1

Cover design by David Carlson Design
Cover image by Tatsuhiko Shimada/Photonica

Scripture quotations are from:
The Holy Bible, New King James Version
© 1984 by Thomas Nelson, Inc.

The Holy Bible, New International Version (NIV)
© 1973, 1984 by International Bible Society,
used by permission of Zondervan Publishing House

Holy Bible, New Living Translation (NLT)
© 1996. Used by permission of Tyndale House Publishers, Inc.
All rights reserved.

The Good News Bible: The Bible in Today's English Version (TEV)
© 1976 by American Bible Society

Multnomah is a trademark of Multnomah Publishers, Inc.
and is registered in the U.S. Patent and Trademark Office.
The colophon is a trademark of Multnomah Publishers, Inc.

Printed in the United States of America

For information:
MULTNOMAH PUBLISHERS, INC.
POST OFFICE BOX 1720
SISTERS, OREGON 97759

01 02 03 04 05—10 9 8 7 6 5 4 3 2 1 0

Introduction

A Prayer to Change Your Life

Sometime around three thousand years ago, one of history's great nobodies decided to pray. When he looked at himself and his circumstances, he saw no reason for hope. But when he prayed, he prayed the boldest, most hopeful prayer he could imagine. And God answered.

God is still answering. The prayer of a man named Jabez is motivating millions of people today to seek the Lord in a new way, to cry out to Him for blessing, and to reach for a larger life in His service. Are you one? Then you too are an answer to Jabez's prayer.

Once you see what God can do through His most ordinary servants, you'll never want to slide back into mediocre living. For too long, Christians have drastically underestimated God's desire to bless them and work through them to accomplish His will in the world.

If Jabez were around today, he'd be quick to tell you that the words of his little prayer hold no magical powers. But he would also tell you that if you want to experience God's greater purpose for your life—no matter how unpromising your circumstances might be right now—you're just a prayer away.

The Little Man with No Future

If you haven't read *The Prayer of Jabez* yet, I highly recommend you do. If you're new to the story, you'll find it in 1 Chronicles, buried in the official genealogies of the tribes of Israel. The historian, writing about 500 B.C., traces the official family tree of the Jews from Adam through thousands of years up to his own time. That endeavor makes for hundreds of names—most of them unfamiliar and hard to pronounce.

Take chapter 4. *The sons of Judah were Perez, Hezron, Carmi, Hur, and Shobal.* And that's just verse one.

Ahumai

Ishma

Idbash

Hazelponi

Anub…

A DIFFERENT KIND OF BIBLE STUDY

The four-week Bible study you're holding invites you to go deeply into God's Word to see how the message of Jabez's little prayer is supported and explained by the whole of Scripture. Besides being biblically based and felt-needs oriented, the study has several key distinctives:

It's topical. We focus on the biblical reasons to pray for blessing, influence, power, and protection so that we can do God's work in the world. You won't find, for example, a book study or an in-depth approach to theology or doctrine.

It's conversation friendly. Some questions are information based. Some are intended simply to provoke a helpful discussion.

It's designed for individual or group use.

It's question driven. Sometimes called the Socratic method, this teaching method pulls you from topic to topic through a sequence of key questions.

It incorporates several learning approaches. You'll find inductive studies, fill-in-the-blanks, personal inventories, character profiles, Bible exposition, activity-based assignments, and inspiring quotes.

It offers optional study plans. The study presents more learning opportunities than a class can complete in an hour. Select the material that will work best for you. Some groups will want to extend this four-part study to an eight- or twelve-week course.

It's all about life change. The whole purpose of studying God's Word is to be changed in our character and our behavior so that we please God more, become more like Christ, and serve Him more every day.

BIBLE VERSION

The study, as well as the book it is based on, has been prepared using the New King James Version of the Bible. Using that version privately or in class will ensure convenience and clarity, but it is not required.

Not exactly suspenseful reading! But midlitany, the chronicler stops. One name deserves special comment:

> Now Jabez was more honorable than his brothers, and his mother called his name Jabez, saying, "Because I bore him in pain." And Jabez called on the God of Israel saying, "Oh, that You would bless me indeed, and enlarge my territory, that Your hand would be with me, and that You would keep me from evil, that I may not cause pain!" So God granted him what he requested. (1 Chronicles 4:9)

HELPING YOU GET AROUND

You'll see three icons used throughout the study to help you use the material more quickly.

 indicates a key verse, definition, or explanation that you won't want to miss.

 indicates optional material for further study. Use this icon to help you decide what materials you can leave for later.

 indicates a group process question that focuses on life experience.

RECOMMENDED RESOURCES

The Prayer of Jabez Audio, read by the author, can provide busy people with an easy way to learn and review the message of the book.

The Prayer of Jabez Devotional (and accompanying *Journal*) by Bruce Wilkinson. This thirty-one-day devotional follows the same four-week structure as the Bible study.

If you are a teenager (or have one in your home), I recommend *The Prayer of Jabez for Teens.* These resources are all available from Multnomah Publishers.

For younger kids, I suggest *The Prayer of Jabez for Kids* (Tommy Nelson).

Visit www.prayerofjabez.com for recent updates on the Jabez phenomenon, new product information, inspiring stories from readers, and help from *Hot Questions, Helpful Answers,* a response forum from the author.

Also watch for the *Prayer of Jabez* videos, coming in 2002.

In the next verse, the roll call continues as if nothing has happened—*Chelub, Shuah, Mehir....* You can scour from front to back in the Bible as I have, looking for more insight into this man Jabez, and you'll find nothing. We know simply that things started badly for a person no one had heard of; he prayed an unusual, one-sentence prayer; and things ended extraordinarily well.

That one prayer and a life that was "more honorable than his brothers" earned Jabez a place of honor in Israel's history books. And fortunately for us, his minibiography reveals an intriguing record of personal transformation. In only two verses, we see cause and effect—beginning, middle, and end. And if we look hard enough, we find hiding behind each of his four requests a truth that can change our lives and our futures.

WHERE MIRACLES BEGIN

Personal change begins when you cry out to God *for what He wants for you* with hands open and heart expectant. Miracles begin here, too. Each day you'll see new beginnings and new opportunities. You'll think new thoughts. The direction and impact of your life will shift. And your name, like Jabez's, will be headed for God's honor roll for all eternity.

As you study from page to page in the days ahead, remember that you are in full pursuit of blessing from a God who can "do exceedingly abundantly above all that we ask or think, according to the power that works in us" (Ephesians 3:20). May He strengthen and guide you—and bless you *indeed!*

God shapes the world by prayer.
Prayers are deathless.
They outlive the lives of those who utter them.

E. M. BOUNDS

Week One

"OH, THAT YOU WOULD BLESS ME INDEED!"

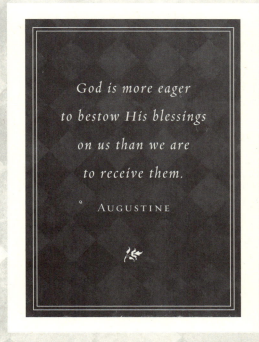

God is more eager
to bestow His blessings
on us than we are
to receive them.

AUGUSTINE

GETTING STARTED

Have you asked God for anything truly impressive lately?

You've probably asked Him to bless the food, bless the kids, bless your day. But when was the last time you asked God for something huge— something that would change your life now and make an impact for all of eternity? To pour out His lovingkindness on you with such bounty that your heart would fill to overflowing?

The first part of the Jabez prayer, "Oh, that You would bless me indeed!" asks God to do something supernatural in your life. Because the only way you can live a blessed life is if God acts.

When you ask God for what He already longs to give you, amazing things start to happen!

THIS WEEK YOU'LL DISCOVER...

♦ what the word *blessing* means.
♦ why you must ask in order to receive certain kinds of blessings.
♦ why it's not selfish to ask God to bless you.
♦ what attitudes need to be revised to agree with the Bible.
♦ how to pray the advanced prayer for the Jabez blessing.

1. What do I really believe about blessing?

1. *Some people feel greatly blessed by God. Others do not. Which category do you fall in, and why?*

My Blessing Inventory

2. *The following inventory will bring to the surface what you believe about God's desire to bless you. Score yourself with the numbers 1 through 5 as follows:* ❶Strongly disagree. ❷Slightly disagree. ❸Unsure. ❹Agree. ❺Strongly agree.

4 I pray every day asking God to bless me.

5 I can quickly recall specific blessings God has given in the past.

2 I think of God as loving and eager to give me blessing.

5 I believe that one reason God hates ongoing sin in my life is because it blocks some of the blessings he wants to give me.

5 I've experienced that the greatest blessings in life grow directly out of my personal relationship with God.

21 YOUR SCORE: Total the values assigned to the five statements. If you scored…

21–25 *You're flying high on the blessings of God.*
16–20 *You're a frequent flyer.*
11–15 *You're hoping to lift off soon.*
5–10 *You need to spread your wings.*

3. *How would you pray differently if you genuinely believed that there are many blessings God gives only to those who ask?*

I would start asking for the blessings that he wants to give me.

"" TALK POINT ""

Growing up, did your family ever openly pray for God's blessings?

Did something happen that makes you feel totally "unblessable"?

Are you emotionally comfortable asking God for His blessing?

2. WHAT DOES GOD'S BLESSING MEAN?

KEY Forms of the verb *to bless* (*barak* in Hebrew) appear nearly four hundred times in the Old Testament. To bless means to favor, honor or bestow special gifts or status. In the Bible, for example, fathers pronounced blessings on their sons to pass along the family birthright or inheritance. People blessed God in their worship—"Bless, the LORD, O my soul, and forget not all His benefits" (Psalm 103:2).

But the kind of blessing we're talking here is God's favor on us—His supernatural gifts that we don't earn and that we can't receive from anyone else. That's why the Bible says, "It is the LORD'S blessing that makes you wealthy. Hard work can make you no richer" (Proverbs 10:22, TEV).

The Bible clearly teaches that God cares about all our needs—material, emotional, and spiritual.

1. *Where do you think your blessings come from? From your family, marriage, job, hard work, or mere chance? Read James 1:16—17. Why is it so easy to become deceived (v. 16) and think we are the source of our blessings?*

2. *Do you think everyone who prospers is being blessed by God? (Psalm 37 records the grief a believer can feel when evildoers prosper.)*

3. *Does God guarantee material blessings and prosperity to believers? Might there be good reasons to withhold them?*

4. *When you receive eternal salvation, God gives you what Paul calls "every spiritual blessing...in Christ" (Ephesians 1:3). Read Ephesians 1:4—14. Write down some spiritual blessings Paul mentions.*

KEY You can also understand blessings in terms of the basis on which they're given:

♦ A *conditional blessing* means there's something I have to do if I want what God has to give. If I don't do it, I won't get the blessings. Check Christ's conditional blessings in Matthew 5:11–12 and the blessings and curses listed in Deuteronomy 28–30.

♦ An *unconditional blessing* is one that God decides to give with no requirements. The recipient doesn't have to qualify to receive it. Look at the promises God made to Abraham in Genesis 12:2–3.

5. *Are the blessings you receive at salvation (described in Ephesians 1) conditional or unconditional blessings, or both?*

6. *One kind of unconditional blessing could be called* <u>compassionate blessings.</u>
KEY *These blessings are based on the nature and character of God. He simply wants to give! (Read Exodus 34:6 to see God's self-portrait.) And it is His will that we want all of what He has to give. What do you learn about God's desire to bless in these verses?*

1 Corinthians 2:9

Romans 8:28–30

Romans 2:4

James 1:17

7. *What kind(s) of blessings do you think Jabez was asking for? What is the basis of your conclusion?*

TALK POINT

What is the greatest blessing you've ever received in your life?

Have you always considered it a blessing?

3. WHO ELSE IN THE BIBLE WAS EXTRAORDINARILY BLESSED?

ABRAHAM: THE MAN GOD CHOSE TO BLESS.
[Read Genesis 12:1–3]

KEY Jabez traced his "blessing inheritance" back to Abraham, the father of the Jewish people. One day God promised Abraham, "I will bless you…and you shall be a blessing" (Genesis 12:2). It was an unconditional covenant of generosity initiated by God.

Abraham believed God and traveled to the Promised Land (Canaan) in pursuit of the blessing. But Abraham didn't earn God's goodness. In fact, if you trace his life story (Genesis 12–25), you'll see a man who made a lot of mistakes. But he never stopped reaching for God's favor. That's why the Bible calls Abraham "friend of God" (James 2:23) and "father of all those who believe" (Romans 4:11).

1. *Abraham saw God as the source of guaranteed blessing. Read Hebrews 11:1, 2, 6, and 8–12. What one thing did Abraham do that pleased God?*

2. *How does a person's faith in God relate to the blessings that he or she receives?*

> **" " TALK POINT " "**
>
> Who in your life is the best example of a person that seems to enjoy God's ongoing blessing?
>
> How do you account for the difference between his or her life and yours?

JACOB: THE MAN WHO WRESTLED TO BE BLESSED.
[Read Genesis 32:22–29]

God renewed His promise of blessing to Abraham's son Isaac (Genesis 26:24) and again to Isaac's son Jacob (35:9). Jacob, whose name meant "schemer" or "grabber," started out his life manipulating others to get ahead. But one night, Jacob came face to face with the real source of blessing. An angelic being met him in the dark, and they wrestled. All night, Jacob struggled to win. By morning, Jacob knew what he was really fighting for. He cried out, "I will not let You go unless You bless me!" (Genesis 32:26).

It was a cry that God was waiting to hear. The angel gave Jacob God's blessing. And Jacob received a new name—Israel, or "prince with God."

3. *How do you think people today struggle and wrestle with God? Why did Jacob wrestle with God before he asked for the blessing?*

4. *What would you have said if you had been Jacob and the angel said to you: "I will bless you! Now, what specific blessing do you want?"*

DAVID: THE MAN WHO UNDERSTOOD THE SOURCE OF BLESSINGS.
[Read 1 Chronicles 29:9−18]

eXTRA The lavish generosity of the Jewish people in donating to the temple highlighted the last days of King David. Perhaps more than any other person in the Old Testament, David understood the profound role of God in this act of sacrificial worship.

5. *List the blessings found in this passage that David reveals come from God.*

6. *Describe the best thing that happened to you in the last three months. Read James 1:17. Did you link it to God's blessing and thank Him for it?*

4. HOW DO I MAXIMIZE GOD'S BLESSINGS?

INSIGHT #1
"It's not selfish to pray, 'Bless me, indeed!'"

For many Christians, the whole idea of praying for personal blessings sounds wrong. *Aren't we supposed to pray for others, not ourselves?* they ask. *Isn't it selfish to ask for me?*

KEY 🔑 Certainly asking for blessing isn't the only way to pray. We're taught to intercede for others, to confess, to worship, and to give thanks. The Jabez prayer simply starts with our urgent desire to receive God's special favor. It is based on a radical trust that God will answer in great love.

For the verses provided below, write out what you discover about God that would encourage you to boldly ask for blessing:

1 JOHN 3:1. *We are God's loved* _____.

ROMANS 8:16–17. *We are not just God's children, but His* _____.

MATTHEW 7:9–11. *Compared to an earthly father who wants to bless his child, our Father is* _____ *to give us good things.*

MATTHEW 7:7–8. *Jesus promised results in our prayers if we* _____, _____ *and* _____.

EPHESIANS 3:20. *God is able to do "* _____ *above all that we ask or think."*

GETTING SPECIFIC

God is pleased when, like Jabez, we trustingly ask Him for His best without specifying exactly how we want Him to bless us. But it's okay to go beyond the Jabez prayer and ask God to bless us in a specific way. Those prayers please the Lord, too. Just be careful to check your motives…and to keep your eyes open for God's surprising answers.

INSIGHT #2

"Blessing doesn't always equal 'health and wealth.'"

Unfortunately, some teach that God wants every believer to prosper materially and that your prosperity proves God's favor. That would mean if you don't have the house and car you want, something is wrong with your faith.

KEY This teaching is a distortion of what the Bible clearly says in 1 Timothy 6:5–10. It also contradicts not only the call of Jesus to take up our crosses and follow Him (Luke 9:23–25), but also His own example of setting aside worldly comforts to do the will of His Father, even to the point of death on the cross (Philippians 2:5–8).

TALK POINT

Can God bless you even when He appears to be saying no to a specific request? _____

_____ How?

So how do we pray for generous blessing without crossing over into God-dishonoring prayer?

JAMES 4:3. *Pray with* _____ *motives.*

1 JOHN 5:14. *Pray according to God's* _____.

MATTHEW 6:33. *Seek* _____ *the kingdom of God.*

1 JOHN 2:15–17. *Make sure that a love for the world and its values has not replaced your* _____ *for God.*

1 TIMOTHY 2:1. *Don't pray just for yourself but for the needs of* _____.

1 CORINTHIANS 10:31. *Evaluate everything you do and want and pray for, and decide if it is something that will bring God* _____.

PHILIPPIANS 3:8–10. *Ask for and pursue a growing relationship with* _____ *so that you can become more like Him.*

5. HOW DO I RECEIVE GOD'S BLESSINGS IN MY LIFE?

It's very simple: Do what Jabez did. He "called on the God of Israel." Even though God has the power to drop every good thing into our lives automatically, He has another plan. His plan is our task. And our task is to ask!

1. *What do these passages tell you about asking?*

    MATTHEW 7:7–11

    PHILIPPIANS 4:19

    JAMES 1:5–8

    HEBREWS 4:14–16

2. *Read Matthew 7:11. What key ingredient is required to be given "good things" by our heavenly Father? How does the prayer of Jabez illustrate what Christ is teaching here?*

3. *One of the most inspiring parts of Jabez's prayer for blessing is the word <u>indeed</u>. Jabez asked for an incredible amount of blessings. Read carefully Ephesians 3:20. How does Paul describe the word <u>indeed</u>?*

"AT LEAST TAKE A BUCKET..."

Asking is the beginning of receiving.
Make sure you don't go to the ocean with a teaspoon.
At least take a bucket so the kids won't laugh at you.

JIM ROHN

6. WHAT WOULD MY LIFE LOOK LIKE IF I ASKED FOR BLESSING?

 Look for clues to the blessed life in these letters from *The Prayer of Jabez* Web site (www.prayerofjabez.com).

Changing the Equation

The great thing about Jabez's prayer is that you are releasing yourself into God's hands and to His will. I think that is what God likes so much. We remove ourselves from the equation and He is unhindered to do exactly what He has always wanted to do. —Unsigned

Selfish Prayer Changes "Selfish Person"

This is ironic—the prayer of Jabez asks for personal blessings, but after reading the book twice and saying the prayer for thirty-six days, I've learned how selfish I am. I've realized that I need to be more understanding and responsive to others at my job before I can help them. I have received blessings, but only after I put others first before myself. I am being molded to be the vessel so I can help the children of God for Him through me! That is a blessing! —Karen

Up and Running

God has gotten my old, raggedy truck up and running, given me more work than I can probably get done, and just simply straightened out many other things. —Wayne

Marriage Set Free

Several years ago, my husband and I were in deep financial trouble, and our marriage had hit bottom. One evening I prayed earnestly that God would bless my marriage and our future. I told the Lord that I knew it was His will that our marriage should be honoring to Him. What followed has astounded me! I won't say it was easy, but as my husband and I regularly asked for God's blessings and watched for them, we were set free. Today we're more in love than when we first married. God has so blessed us financially that we were able to provide our parents with a car and a dear friend a down payment on a home. God is so good! —Unsigned

7. WHAT IS KEEPING ME FROM BREAKING THROUGH TO THE BLESSED LIFE?

Jabez began his life with a handicap—"And his mother called his name Jabez, saying, 'Because I bore him in pain.'"

KEY Yet Jabez didn't let a hurtful past or an unpromising present keep him from asking God for a huge blessing.

Did you begin your life with a disadvantage? Have you faced shame and rejection? Do you feel like a nobody? Negative life experiences can profoundly influence how we see ourselves and how we understand and relate to God. They can change the way we pray, cutting us off from His abundant best.

Do you recognize yourself in any of the attitudes or beliefs listed below?

"" TALK POINT ""

If Jesus came to you and said, "I will bless you greatly and change the world through you, but...you must make sacrifices for Me," what would you say?
(see Acts 9:10—16)

How?

❏ Yes ❏ No   1. TRAPPED. *"I feel cursed. I feel trapped between a bad past and a bleak future."*

❏ Yes ❏ No   2. AFRAID. *"Actually, I'm afraid of too much blessing. God might turn my life upside down. What if I can't handle it?"*

❏ Yes ❏ No   3. UNWORTHY. *"Why would He bless me when I don't deserve it? I need to get my act together first."*

❏ Yes ❏ No   4. UNLOVABLE. *"I'm unlovable. God might love me a little bit, but like me enough to really bless me? I don't think so!"*

❏ Yes ❏ No   5. SKEPTICAL. *"I'm not sure that God is that involved, especially in everything in my little life."*

If one or more of these statements describes how you think or feel, a lie is robbing you of blessings. Read the truth in the references below. Then paraphrase the truth as a new breakthrough belief for your life.

1. TRAPPED? Read 2 Corinthians 5:17; 2 Corinthians 4:16–18;
    1 Corinthians 6:9–10.
    My new breakthrough belief is that I'm not trapped. In fact,...

2. AFRAID? Read 2 Timothy 1:7; Hebrews 13:5–6; Romans 9:37–39;
    Matthew 6:25–30.
    Even when I feel afraid, my new breakthrough belief is...

3. UNWORTHY? Read Colossians 1:13–14; Galatians 4:4–6;
    Ephesians 2:8–10.
    My new breakthrough belief is that, far from being unworthy, I'm...

4. UNLOVABLE? Read John 3:16–17; 1 John 3:1–2;
    Romans 8:15–17.
    My new breakthrough belief is that God loves me—and likes me—because...

5. SKEPTICAL? Read Proverbs 3:5–6; Philippians 1:6;
    Matthew 10:29–31.
    I can let go of my doubts because my new breakthrough belief is...

MY NEW START IN THE BLESSED LIFE

To close this study on blessing, pray the following prayer aloud together. Then pray it on your own every day in the coming week.

My Prayer for Blessing

Dear Lord,
I want every single blessing
that You would love to give me.
Forgive me for not desiring
these enough to ask for them.
Please open Your heart, and be gracious to me.
You are good, and everything You do is good.
So let me experience You today,
in all of your abundant lovingkindness,
even though I am in all of my unworthiness.
Touch my life in ways that are very personal
so that I don't miss Your fingerprints.
Bless me, Lord, I pray—bless me, indeed!
And I will praise You, from whom
all blessings flow.
Amen.

God be merciful to me and bless me, and cause Your face to shine upon me,
That Your way may be known on earth, Your salvation among all nations.

FROM PSALM 67:1–2

Week Two

"OH, THAT YOU WOULD ENLARGE MY TERRITORY!"

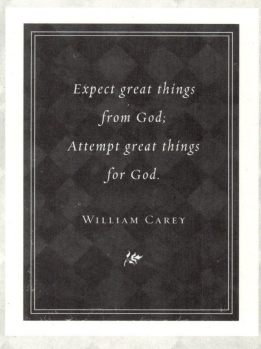

*Expect great things
from God;
Attempt great things
for God.*

WILLIAM CAREY

BORN FOR MORE

If your circumstances often seem ordinary and your horizons small, you're going to love the next part of the Jabez prayer.

For his second request, Jabez pleaded for more territory. With more influence and more responsibility, Jabez could make a greater mark for the God of Israel. But he was stuck on a tiny patch of opportunity. So he asked for more.

As you enjoy more and more of God's blessings in your life, your heart will overflow, touching more and more people for Him. Most people live their lives in a passive, reactive mode; Jabez lived in a healthy, proactive mode. Jabez stepped forward and boldly asked God to enlarge his borders and extend his influence.

Do you believe that God wants you to have more and do more for Him? I do. But asking for a larger life goes far beyond the size of your property, as you're about to find out.

THIS WEEK YOU'LL DISCOVER...

♦ what *territory* means.
♦ why God wants you to have more of it.
♦ how other Bible characters enlarged their territory.
♦ how God arranges divine encounters between you and others.
♦ what might be fencing you in on a small patch of opportunity.
♦ how to break through to a larger life every day.

1. AM I A "BOUNDARY BUSTER"?

1. *Many Christians aren't sure that they are called to be a strategic part of what God is doing in the world. In quiet moments of introspection, they wonder if maybe they were born benchwarmers instead of boundary busters. A few know that God has called them to much more. If benchwarmers became convinced that they were boundary busters, how would it change their lives?*

MY TERRITORY INVENTORY

2. *Take a fresh look at your behavior—are you ready to step up for a larger life for God? Score yourself using this standard:* ❶ No, not yet. ❷ Rarely, if ever. ❸ Sometimes. ❹ Quite often. ❺ Yes, regularly.

____ I feel restless to take on greater challenges for God.

____ I ask God to enlarge the size and scope of my personal influence for Him.

____ I watch out for potential areas where I might minister to others.

____ I overcome my initial fears when faced with a new ministry opportunity.

____ I am ready to make significant personal sacrifices in order to touch this world for God.

____ YOUR SCORE: Total the values assigned to the five statements. If you scored…

21—25 *You're eager to take new territory for God.*
16—20 *You're checking out some travel brochures.*
11—15 *You're not opposed to a walk around the block.*
5—10 *You need to get out more!*

"" TALK POINT ""

How could a person who is already feeling busy or overwhelmed enlarge his or her life for God?

Does pursuing more influence or significance always mean doing more?

2. WHAT DOES *TERRITORY* MEAN— AND WHERE IS MINE?

KEY Depending on the Bible version you're reading, the word *territory* in 1 Chronicles 4:10 may also be translated as *borders* or *coast*. In Jabez's time, the more land you had, the more provisions, security, and influence you enjoyed. I believe that Jabez desired to enlarge his territory because as an honorable man he wanted more opportunity to make a mark for the God of Israel.

Like Jabez, we have territory—many spheres of influence that overflow with unlimited opportunities. This territory includes all those whose lives we touch, whether in family, church, business, school, or community. In the same way that God blesses us for a purpose, He is ready to expand our territory for a purpose—so we will have more influence for Him.

1.   *List three areas of influence where you have the most potential impact. Then list one person in each area that you are in a position to influence most.*

2.   *Describe how you feel about the size and scope of your territory right now. If God enlarged it today, where do you wish He would start, and why?*

SPHERES OF INFLUENCE

KEY When we're ready to enlarge our territory for God, He helps us move outward through the *spheres of influence* we already have:

♦ Start with family and friends,
♦ move out to neighborhood and community,
♦ jump to new places, people, and cultures,
♦ ask for planet earth.

3. How does this pattern match up with Jesus' plan for the early church as described in Acts 1:8?

THE M WORD

KEY My favorite word for enlarging my territory is *ministry*. Ministry describes what happens when God uses you to help or influence others for Him. You could say that the Jabez Real Estate Law for Christians is: *My territory = my spheres of influence = my potential ministry.*

4. The New Testament teaches that all believers—not just preachers, teachers, and evangelists—are called to serve God in ministry (Acts 13:2; Ephesians 4:11). Take note of God's provisions for you:

    1 PETER 2:9–10. *Every believer is a high priest to proclaim His* _____ .

    MATTHEW 28:18–20. *Every believer is commissioned to make* _____ .

    ACTS 1:8. *Every believer receives power from the* _____ .

    1 CORINTHIANS 12:4–11. *Every believer has been given a spiritual* _____ .

    EPHESIANS 2:10. *Every believer is created for specific good* _____ .

5. God carefully crafted you for a specific purpose. When you pray for God to enlarge your ministry, He usually matches opportunities to your gifts and talents. If you were to describe the way the Lord could use you most effectively for Him, what would it be?

" " **TALK POINT** " "

When was the last time you asked God for more ministry?

What happened?

3. WHAT DOES THE BIBLE SAY ABOUT TAKING TERRITORY FOR GOD?

THE GREATEST "TERRITORY STORY" EVER TOLD.
Part 1 (Old Testament)

KEY The Bible is composed of two testaments (Old and New) about two peoples (Jews and Christians), but it has one overriding message: God seeks a people to worship and serve Him by bringing His salvation to the world. The Abrahamic covenant (Genesis 12:1–3) reveals God's missionary heart to reach all nations through His people, the Jews, and ultimately His Son, Jesus Christ (see Galatians 3:8).

1. *Why do you think God wanted the whole nation to be His missionaries rather than only a select group of paid ministers? Did they fulfill His wish?*

> **" " TALK POINT " "**
>
> Look around: What is the territory that would be the most challenging to take for the Lord?

2. *Why didn't God just give the Israelites the Promised Land without them having to fight for it? How does that relate to our taking territory for Him today?*

"I HAVE SET THE LAND BEFORE YOU..."
OLD TESTAMENT

"See, I have set the land before you; go in and possess the land which the LORD swore to your fathers—to Abraham, Isaac, and Jacob—to give to them and their descendants after them." DEUTERONOMY 1:8

THE GREATEST "TERRITORY STORY" EVER TOLD.

Part 2 (New Testament)

KEY In the New Testament, the focus shifts from reaching the world through the Jewish nation to reaching the world through the church—those who have come to know Jesus Christ as their personal Savior, without regard to nation or race. "For God so loved the world…" Jesus told Nicodemus (John 3:16).

Talk about expanded borders! Jesus Christ came to die for the sins of the world (Luke 19:10). Now, instead of possessing land for God's glory, our mission is to "Go…and make disciples of all nations."

3.   *Often when we desire to do more for God, we feel great chains holding us back from moving forward. How could you get free?*

" " TALK POINT " "

How does knowing that Jesus *commands* you to take territory change the way you think about this part of the Jabez prayer?

2.   *The New Testament equivalent of opposition from hostile tribes is persecution. What persecution have you or your church faced, and how did you respond?*

"MAKE DISCIPLES OF ALL NATIONS…"

NEW TESTAMENT

"Go therefore and make disciples of all the nations, baptizing them in the name of the Father and of the Son and of the Holy Spirit, teaching them to observe all things that I have commanded you; and lo, I am with you always, even to the end of the age."

MATTHEW 28:19–20

4. HOW COULD GOD WORK THROUGH ME TO REACH OTHERS?

KEY God has plans to help you reach across boundary lines and touch lives for Him. I call them Jabez Appointments. They occur when you respond to what seems to be a divinely arranged encounter...and you invite God to act. Often, your appointment starts with a simple question: "How may I help you?"

CASE STUDY #1

Philip—a Jabez Appointment in a chariot.

[Read Acts 8:26–39]

Directed by an angel, Philip traveled into the desert for a Jabez Appointment with an Ethiopian government official. The official was traveling by chariot back to Africa. Without this miraculously arranged appointment, the Ethiopian official, who had come to Jerusalem in search of God, would have returned home without hearing the gospel.

1. *Since timing is important in encounters, what can you learn from Philip's response as soon as he received the angel's message (Acts 8:27)?*

2. *How did Philip's willingness to keep his desert appointment consequently affect the Ethiopian (vv. 37–39)?*

PHILIP'S ROADSIDE OPPORTUNITY

So Philip ran to him, and heard him reading the prophet Isaiah, and said, "Do you understand what you are reading?" And [the Ethiopian] said, "How can I, unless someone guides me?" And he asked Philip to come up and sit with him. ACTS 8:30–31

CASE STUDY #2

Peter—a Jabez Appointment on a rooftop.

[Read Acts 10]

eXTRA A Gentile soldier named Cornelius wants to know more about God. With the help of an angel and a very alarming dream, God brought Cornelius and Peter together. The results: A family came to faith in Christ, a believer expanded his boundaries (and his understanding of God's love), and the church broke through an ancient boundary line of prejudice.

3. *Cornelius is a perfect example of a man seeking God. From Acts 10:1—4, 22, 30—34, list his behaviors that reveal his hunger for God.*

" " TALK POINT " "

When have you felt most sure that you were keeping an appointment with someone for God?

What did God do through you?

What could you learn from it?

4. *Sometimes we don't know what to say to a seeker like Cornelius. Peter's minimessage is user-friendly. Outline his points in Acts 10:34—43.*

5. *Can you find Peter's "How may I help you?" question?*

PETER'S BIG "AHA!"

"How beautiful are the feet of those who preach the gospel of peace, who bring glad tidings of good things!"

ROMANS 10:15

5. WHAT WOULD MY LIFE LOOK LIKE IF GOD ENLARGED MY BORDERS?

e-XTRA The letters on these pages are from *The Prayer of Jabez* Web site (www.prayerofjabez.com). Browse through them for territory-taking pointers about…

♦ how God works;
♦ how God uses us even without much experience;
♦ how quickly God might answer your prayer for more territory;
♦ when and where you might meet a Jabez Appointment;
♦ how you'll feel when you know you've had one.

STRAP YOURSELF IN!

The prayer of Jabez should come with seat belts! It is a wild ride! Since I have prayed Jabez a flood of atheists have been e-mailing me, calling me, working for me, and bumping into me in the middle of the night in a faraway town. I've never talked about Jesus with more atheists in my entire life! I am not sure why I'm getting the advanced series witnessing jobs from my Father, but I trust that He knows what He's doing in His perfect plan laid out for my life! —Mark

UNBELIEVABLE?

As I read your book, I started to pray immediately that God would expand our borders. But before I even finished the book, I got an e-mail from a reporter at USA Today *saying she had happened to find our Web site and wondered if she could do a feature story about our ministry in her paper! I had to hurry up and read the rest of your book to find out what to do next! Unbelievably (in human terms),* USA Today *ran a half-page story that not only featured our ministry, but clearly and graciously pointed people back to God and the Bible for the solutions to their problems.* —Eric

WAITING FOR A PURPOSE

I have asked for a blessing each day since reading your book and have received one or more each day. For example, while in a hospital waiting room I happened to sit next to a woman whose husband was undergoing cancer surgery. We began a conversation. She really needed someone to listen to her. Even as we were talking, I felt blessed and knew that the Lord was enlarging my territory. Later, she said she felt the Lord had sent me to be with her at this time. —Unsigned

"I'M AN INTROVERT..."

Last Tuesday, a woman in a doctor's office began to make small talk about her family. I asked where her daughter lived. I found out that she lived one street over from me and that she didn't know the Lord. After I prayed with her, the woman looked up at me with tear-filled eyes and said, "You know that God meant for us to meet here today." Oh, yes, ma'am, I absolutely know that! The funny thing is, I am an introvert who has always found it hard to talk to people I don't know. I guess God doesn't know that! —Unsigned

WHAT WILL GOD DO NEXT?

Early this morning, I prayed for more territory. As soon as I got to work I received a phone call from a lady asking me to serve on a board that oversees a mentoring group that strives to keep teens in school. Immediately, God spoke in my spirit that He was enlarging my circle of influence and would give me opportunities to minister in His name. What will God do next? —Jay

YOU NEED A MIRACLE TODAY

A Jabez Appointment is a miracle. It occurs when God moves supernaturally to arrange circumstances and bring people together so that your ministry can be expanded. Miracles aren't magic and don't always break the laws of nature, but they require God's intervention. For instance, when Christ calmed the storm, no law of nature was broken. Only the timing of the end of the storm changed. When Christ provided Peter with a huge catch of fish, no law of nature was broken, but God supernaturally brought fish and Peter's net together.

God is ready to answer your prayer for a Jabez Miracle. He will...

♦ arrange your day so you connect with the right person,
♦ give you words to say when you can't think of any,
♦ provide wisdom you didn't know you had,
♦ give you boldness when you feel fear,
♦ bring to mind key Scriptures related to the situation.

6. WHAT KEEPS ME FROM REACHING FOR MORE TERRITORY?

KEY Borders. Limits. Comfort zones. We all have them—invisible lines we don't want to cross. Why? Because we think the really good life is on *this side* of the line, where everything is safe and known. But think about it: Doesn't God sometimes heap blessings on your life so that you can't wait to step across that line to tell someone about God's love?

Do you recognize yourself in any of the limiting attitudes or beliefs listed below?

BARBED WIRE THINKING THAT FENCES ME IN

❏ Yes ❏ No 1. <u>SHY</u>. *"I'm afraid of new people and new situations. Can I take territory for God from the safety of my couch?"*

❏ Yes ❏ No 2. <u>UNGIFTED</u>. *"I'm so ordinary that I'm practically invisible. And I don't have special gifts. How can God make me an influence for Him?"*

❏ Yes ❏ No 3. <u>AFRAID TO FAIL</u>. *"I'm afraid God will take me outside my comfort zone, then I'll get in too deep and blow it. And I hate to fail."*

❏ Yes ❏ No 4. <u>RELUCTANT TO SURRENDER CONTROL</u>. *"If I let go of control, I worry about what God will do to me—send me to the worst place on earth? Make me give away my prized possessions? Ask me to talk to my stepmom?"*

❏ Yes ❏ No 5. <u>OVEREXTENDED</u>. *"I don't have the time or resources. In fact, I'm already too busy."*

ONE JUMP

Don't be afraid to take a big step.
You can't cross a chasm in two small jumps.

DAVID LLOYD GEORGE

If one or more of these statements describes how you think or feel, a lie is robbing you of the larger life God longs to give you. Read the truth in the references below. Then paraphrase the truth as a new breakthrough belief for your life.

WIRE-CUTTERS, FENCE-BUSTERS, & NEW HORIZON-MAKERS

1. SHY? Read Proverbs 29:25; Jeremiah 1:6–8; 2 Timothy 1:7; Hebrews 13:6.

   My new breakthrough belief is...

2. UNGIFTED? Read 1 Corinthians 1:26–29; 2 Corinthians 4:7; 12:6–7; Romans 12:5–8.

   My new breakthrough belief is...

3. AFRAID TO FAIL? Read Psalm 18:28–36; Nahum 1:7; Matthew 10:18–20.

   My new breakthrough belief is...

4. RELUCTANT TO SURRENDER CONTROL? Read Romans 12:1; Proverbs 3:5–6; Psalm 27:1; 37:3–7; 56:3–4; Hebrews 11:1, 6.

   My new breakthrough belief is...

5. OVEREXTENDED? Read Matthew 11:28–30; Isaiah 40:29–31; Mark 10:27; Philippians 4:12–13; Hebrews 10:35–38.

   My new breakthrough belief is...

MY NEW START IN A LARGER LIFE

To close this study on expanding our territory, pray the following prayer aloud together. Then pray it on your own every day in the coming week.

My Prayer for Territory

Dear Lord,
Thank You for making me in Your image
and for preparing me for a wonderful
and important destiny.
Forgive me for withdrawing into my own
meager and limiting dreams.
When I do this, I deny You the freedom
to use me as Your mouth, hands, and heart.
I want to fulfill Your world-sized dream for me
every day of my life.
And in eternity, I want to run into Your arms
hearing the words, "Well done!"
Please expand my influence and impact for You
beyond all I can imagine.
I am Your devoted servant.
Here I am, Lord, please send me!
Amen.

Also I heard the voice of the Lord, saying: "Whom shall I send, and who will go for Us?" Then I said, "Here am I! Send me."

ISAIAH 6:8

Week Three

"OH, THAT YOUR HAND WOULD BE WITH ME!"

You never become truly spiritual by sitting down and wishing to become so. You must undertake something so great that you cannot accomplish it unaided.

PHILLIPS BROOKS

IT'S TIME TO SINK OR SWIM

Have you ever taken on a big task only to discover too late that you've gotten in *way over your head?*

When you ask God for more blessings and more territory, you'll have that experience. You'll feel like you set out to dog-paddle across your favorite pool only to end up in the middle of the English Channel.

Jabez knew that feeling. That's why in the third part of his prayer he cried out: "Oh, that Your hand would be with me!"

Yet for the Christian, realizing our desperate need for supernatural power is a point of great promise. It's the threshold to the kind of living that changes lives and impacts the world for God. And that's exactly what God has in mind for you.

THIS WEEK YOU'LL DISCOVER...

♦ what it means to have *God's hand* upon you.
♦ why feeling "in over your head" is normal—and what you should do about it.
♦ what the Bible says about being filled with God's Spirit.
♦ what might be keeping you from asking for God's hand upon you.
♦ how you can experience God's power in your life today.

1. HOW MUCH DO I EXPERIENCE GOD'S POWER?

1. *One of the most remarkable teachings of the Bible is that the hand of Almighty God can rest upon a person and provide all the power and resources that are needed to accomplish His will. Describe a time in your life when you either felt or witnessed God's hand powerfully moving. What happened?*

MY POWER INVENTORY

2. *How much do you count on God's hand moving on your behalf as your territory expands for Him? Put a number from 1 through 5 as follows:*
    ❶ Strongly disagree. ❷ Slightly disagree. ❸ Unsure. ❹ Agree. ❺ Strongly agree.

____ Whenever I sense that God is directing me, I'm confident that He has His glory and my good in mind, no matter what I'm feeling at the moment.

____ When I feel inadequate in a ministry situation, I understand that this is a feeling experienced by many who want to take territory for God.

____ I ask fervently and often for God to fill me with His Spirit and power.

____ I believe that doing God's work means I must be willing to attempt things that could require God to intervene.

____ I believe that God stands ready to unleash His power, including miracles, in the lives of believers today.

> **" " TALK POINT " "**
>
> People today place a high value on being self-sufficient. Do you sense that this attitude affects how you live out your faith?
>
> If so, how?
>
> _____

YOUR SCORE: Total the values assigned to the five statements. If you scored…

21–25 *You're destined to overcome the impossible.*
16–20 *You're likely to achieve the unlikely.*
11–15 *You're hoping to achieve the achievable.*
5–10 *You need a new challenge.*

2. WHAT DOES GOD'S "HAND UPON ME" MEAN?

KEY In the Bible, the "hand of God" usually represents the power and/or presence of God in a specific situation or upon a specific person. If God's hand was on someone, He wanted him or her to succeed at what he or she was doing, and He intervened to make it happen. One thing is evident as you read through the Old and New Testaments—God was personally involved in the lives of His children.

1. *What do these Old Testament passages tell you about how God intervenes for His people?*

   EXODUS 6:6–7

   NUMBERS 11:21–23

   2 CHRONICLES 30:12

   EZRA 7:27–28

   NEHEMIAH 2:7–8

2. *If you were convinced that the hand of God was on you, how might you respond differently in a challenging situation (see Nehemiah 2:20)?*

3. *If you saw God's power work through you in such a way that you knew God did that! No one else could have! how would you feel? Would it change what you attempted for God next time around?*

"You Shall Receive Power..."

KEY As you trace the "hand of God" from the Old Testament into the New, a dramatic shift is immediately noticeable. The power of God still intervenes on every page, but the description "hand of God" changes to "Spirit of God." As Jesus prophesied (John 14:16–17, 26; 15:26–27; 16:7–14), the Holy Spirit would abide in His disciples as the hand of God rested upon them. (In Acts 11:21 the "hand of God" is used interchangeably with the "Spirit of God.") That means that when a Christian prays "that Your hand would be with me," you are really asking for the power of the Spirit of God.

4. *According to the following passages, what supernatural resources are available to every believer through the Holy Spirit?*

Acts 1:8. *Supernatural power to be a* _____ *for Christ.*

Acts 16:6–7. *Supernatural* _____.

Romans 8:13. *Supernatural power to put* _____.

Romans 8:16. *Supernatural confirmation we are* _____.

Romans 8:26–27. *Supernatural* _____ *on our behalf.*

1 Corinthians 2:10–12. *Supernatural understanding of the* _____ .

1 Corinthians 12:7–9. *Supernatural* _____ *for ministry.*

Galatians 5:22–23. *Supernatural* _____ *in our character.*

" " TALK POINT " "

Which of these gifts have you experienced most?

Which would you like to ask God to experience more of?

3. WHO ELSE IN THE BIBLE EXPERIENCED GOD'S HAND UPON THEM?

GIDEON, PART 1: A HERO COMES OUT OF HIDING.
[Read Judges 6:1–16]

To deliver Israel from oppression by Midianite raiders, God chooses a man name Gideon. When the angel arrives to tell Gideon the news, Gideon is threshing wheat inside a winepress for fear that enemies will see his harvest and steal it. Yet the angel greets him with the words, "The LORD is with you, you mighty man of valor!" (v. 12).

1. *Why do you suppose the angel called Gideon a "mighty man of valor" when he was behaving so fearfully?*

2. *Why might God choose the weakest man instead of the greatest for a task? (see 1 Corinthians 1:18–31).*

3. *Have you ever felt the way Gideon did when God asked you to do something (see Jude 6:13–15)? How did you respond?*

4. *God had allowed the Midianites to dominate Israel because of her sin (see vv. 25–35). Is it possible that sin in your life is keeping God from showing you His true power?*

"" TALK POINT ""

Read Judges 6:36–40. Is it okay to ask God f or confirmation about what you think He's saying?

Are there times when it might be displeasing to God?

Gideon, Part 2: A Weakling Goes to War.

[Read Judges 7]

When Gideon finally feels ready to go with his army to war, God does the unexpected—He whittles down Gideon's army from thirty-two thousand men to only three hundred.

5. *Look at Judges 7:2–4, then note the size of the enemy army (v. 12). What important truth does this story illustrate about how the "hand of the Lord" may work? What is God trying to prevent (see v. 2)?*

> **"" TALK POINT ""**
>
> Have you ever been in a position where you already felt inadequate, then God asks you to become *even more so?*
>
> What happened?

6. *How can it be true that God gives the victory and yet we have to fight the war (see 7:2)?*

Courage for Cowards

eXTRA Don't miss how God cared about Gideon's need for reassurances. Look for nine encouraging messages or actions. Write down what you think God wanted Gideon to understand in each.

Judges 6:12 With God, I can be brave and strong.	6:14	6:16
6:18	6:21	6:23
6:38	6:40	7:10–11

WHO ELSE IN THE BIBLE...? *(continued)*

KEY As with Gideon's example in the Old Testament, we see a similar pattern at work in the New Testament:
♦ God chooses ordinary people for an impossible mission.
♦ God provides His resources and supernatural power.
♦ With God's power, ordinary people accomplish the impossible (yet they remain ordinary people).

PETER: A FISHERMAN GOES FOR THE BIG ONES

Within a few pages, you can witness what happens to an unpredictable fisherman named Peter after he receives the power of the Holy Spirit (Acts 1:8; 2:1–4) to expand the territory of the church.

1. *Peter preaches boldly (Acts 2:36–41). The disciple who had deserted his Lord only weeks earlier (John 18:15–18) becomes the church's first mass evangelist. What is the extraordinary result (Acts 2:41)? Do you think God still desires such results?*

2. *Peter heals a crippled man (Acts 3:1–10). How did Peter make it clear that the power for healing did not come from him (v. 6)?*

3. *Acts 4 reveals the two secrets that all who pray the Jabez prayer for God's hand must understand.*
   ACTS 4:5–13 *Power is based on our relationship to* _____.
   ACTS 4:31 *Power is received by the filling of the* _____.

4. *Jesus says, "Get the picture?" Now loop back and read John 21:1–11. What lessons about God's power for ministry do you think Jesus was trying to share with Peter and the others that morning on the beach?*

4. How would my life change if I asked for more of God's Spirit?

Browse these letters from www.prayerofjabez.com for hints on how God might want to release His power through you.

Stopping a Tragedy

I received a phone call from a suicidal woman. I didn't know that she had already stabbed her grandson with a knife and was determined to "take them all home with her." But God used me to prevent this tragedy, and we were able to get her the help she needed and save the lives of her grandchildren. What an awesome responsibility God placed in my lap! I was able to get through it successfully, and I saw His hand at work every step of the way. —Cindy

Strength for More

When I entered high school last year, I asked God to use me to my fullest, and I feel that He has. He has placed me in many leadership positions in my church and school. But after He gave me those chances to "expand my horizon," I became overwhelmed and didn't want to go on. But last night, I rededicated my life. Today I went out, praying for His will to be done. I had many opportunities today to reach out to others. My mother even listened to the Word after ten years of trying. Now I realize I can do even more as He gives me the strength to do it. —Justin

Turning Little into Much

It certainly seems strange that a senior pastor of a large, growing church would be so foolish to believe that leaving that congregation and starting over with forty-five people would be the way to touch the world. Yet that is what God is calling me to do. He has a wonderful way of taking little and turning it into much, of taking the ordinary and turning it into the extraordinary. —Forrest

5. HOW DO I EXPERIENCE THE FILLING OF THE SPIRIT?

KEY If you've received Christ as your personal Savior, then the Bible teaches that you have received the Holy Spirit. In fact, Romans 8:9 states that you cannot be a true Christian without the Holy Spirit. The Bible not only invites you to seek a deeper relationship with Jesus Christ, but also to be filled to a greater degree with the Holy Spirit. Why? To do extraordinary works for God, you need to be filled with more of His power.

PART I: WHAT EXACTLY IS THE FILLING OF THE SPIRIT?

The Holy Spirit is a person, and at salvation, you receive Him completely, not partially. The book of Acts recounts the fact that the early Christians were filled repeatedly. When we are willing to let the Holy Spirit saturate us, He pervades our entire being with His presence and power. The filling is not having more of the Holy Spirit, but the Holy Spirit having all of us.

SPIRIT-WISE QUIZ:

1. *Whose responsibility is it that I am filled with the Spirit?*
   A] mine B] my pastor's C] a TV preacher's D] God's E] it just happens

2. *Who actually does the filling?*
   A] me B] my pastor C] a TV preacher D] God E] it just happens

3. *Peter prayed again for filling in Acts 4:31 because:*
   A] the first time didn't work B] he needed to be filled again for another big task C] just a formality D] he needed to get saved again E] don't know

4. *The main reason for being filled with the Holy Spirit is:*
   A] power to impress B] powerful feelings C] power to do tricks D] power to get what I want E] power to speak to others about God and His Word

5. *If I were to pick one word that is used repeatedly to describe how the disciples spoke for God after being filled with the Spirit, I would say that they were:*
   A] cautious B] confused C] rude D] bold E] scared

ANSWERS: 1.A; 2.D; 3.B; 4.E; 5.D

Part 2: How Can I Be Filled with the Spirit?

Although the Bible doesn't give us specifics on how to be filled with the Spirit, many have found these five steps helpful.

Step 1: Recognize When You Need to Be Filled.

In the book of Acts, the disciples repeatedly asked the Spirit to fill them. The reason? They lacked the power and boldness to do the ministry God was giving them. Similarly, if you lack boldness or power to minister, it's time to ask for a new filling. Ephesians 5:18 commands us to keep on being filled.

Step 2: Confess Your Sins and Cleanse Yourself.

Believers can grieve and quench the Spirit through disobedience. Before asking God to fill you, confess your sins (1 John 1:9; 2 Timothy 2:19–22). Get back into an intimate relationship with Jesus Christ.

Step 3: Ask the Spirit of God to Fill You for Service.

The Lord does filling of the Spirit, and you need to pray and ask Him (see Acts 4:31). The Spirit (re)fills believers in response to prayer. Acts 4:31 states, "When they had prayed...they were all filled."

Step 4: Identify What the Spirit Wants Done.

The filling of the Spirit is not the same as the "fruit of the Spirit" or "walking by the Spirit." Filling is specifically given so that you can do His work (Acts 4:29–31). Ask for clarity about what He wants done.

" " TALK POINT " "

Has any of this teaching changed the way you think about the filling of the Holy Spirit? If so, how?

Which of the steps described here do you find the most challenging, and why?

Step 5: Act in Faith in the Power of the Spirit.

Right after the disciples prayed, the Spirit filled them, and they "spoke the word of God with boldness" (Acts 4:31). Believe that God heard your prayer and that you are filled. Then step out immediately to do the work of ministry in His power.

6. WHAT IS KEEPING ME FROM EXPERIENCING GOD'S HAND ?

KEY If you're ready to break through to experiencing the hand of God on your life, try to identify what misconceptions hold you back:

❏ Yes ❏ No 1. IT'S NOT FOR ME. *I think the Spirit is a mysterious power that spiritual people have but that isn't available to me.*

❏ Yes ❏ No 2. I CAN'T COUNT ON GOD'S POWER. *When I get in a place where I can't succeed without supernatural help, I always pull out. I doubt that God will come through for me, and why should I go down in flames?*

❏ Yes ❏ No 3. I CAN'T GET MORE OF GOD'S POWER. *I don't believe you have to ask for more of the Spirit. Every Christian has the power of the Spirit in equal measure at all times.*

❏ Yes ❏ No 4. I'M AFRAID OF LOSING CONTROL. *If I let God's Spirit really work through me, I might do or say crazy things.*

❏ Yes ❏ No 5. I CAN HANDLE IT ON MY OWN. *God gave me abilities, resources, and experience for a reason. God expects me to put them to work, and He'll add His blessing if I do. That's all there is to it.*

If one or more of these statements describes how you think or feel, you're trying to do God's work in your own (very limited) power. Find the truth in the references below. Then paraphrase your new breakthrough belief.

1. IT'S NOT FOR ME. Read Romans 8:9, 15–17; Ephesians 5:18; 1 Corinthians 12:7.
   The supernatural power of the Spirit is available for every believer—including me—because...

2. I CAN'T COUNT ON GOD'S POWER. Read Ephesians 3:20; Colossians 1:28–29; Acts 4:31.
   I can trust God to come through with His power because...

3. I CAN'T GET MORE OF GOD'S POWER. Read Ephesians 1:19–20; 3:16–21; 6:10–20.
   God wants me to ask for more of the Holy Spirit because...

4. I'M AFRAID OF LOSING CONTROL. Read Galatians 5:22–23 (a fruit of the Spirit is self-control—those who are most filled demonstrate most self-control); 1 Corinthians 14:33; 2 Corinthians 3:17.
   My fears of doing or saying strange things when God releases His power through me are groundless because...

5. I CAN HANDLE IT ON MY OWN. Read John 15:5; Zechariah 4:6; 2 Corinthians 3:5–6; 1 Corinthians 2:3–4.
   No matter how smart, talented, or good-looking I am, I still need God's power to do God's work because...

MY NEW START EXPERIENCING GOD'S POWER

To close this study on asking for God's power, pray the following prayer aloud together. Then pray it on your own every day in the coming week.

My Prayer for Power

Dear Lord,
When Your hand has moved in my life
I have seen a glimpse of heaven on earth.
Forgive me for my independent attitude
of believing that I have the power to do Your work.
I beseech You to reach down from the heavens
and put Your mighty hand upon me.
I need and earnestly desire Your strength
working in me, through me,
and around me to do Your work.
So I empty myself and ask You to lavishly fill me
with the full power of Your Spirit
and the glory of Your presence.
By Your hand, I will walk boldly today,
carrying Your light in this dark world.
Amen.

I pray that you... may be filled to the measure of all the fullness of God.

Now to him who is able to do immeasurably more than all we ask or imagine,

according to his power that is at work within us, to him be glory...!

EPHESIANS 3:17, 19–20, NIV

Week Four

"Keep me from evil."

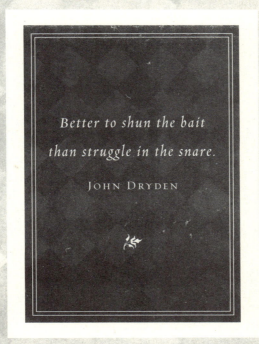

Better to shun the bait

than struggle in the snare.

John Dryden

SECURITY MEASURES

After three border-busting requests, the last request in the Jabez prayer reaches for safety, protection, and long-term security—"Oh, Lord, keep me from evil!"

The request makes a lot of sense. When you're hugely blessed by God, you have a lot to lose. Besides, when you're taking territory *for* God by His power, you are taking it *from* someone else. And the evil one doesn't like it. With God's hand using you in mighty ways for Him, you will become a larger target for the enemy.

That's why Jabez's prayer to be kept from evil is so important.

THIS WEEK YOU'LL DISCOVER...

- what *keep me from evil* means.
- why you should pray to be kept from evil.
- where temptation comes from.
- what the Bible has to say about God's powerful resources for Christians under attack.
- how you can escape temptation when it hits and protect God's blessings in your life.

"Am I a fool for temptation?"

1. *Many Christians think that the more they know about God and the more active they are for Him, the less they'll be tempted. Do you agree? Why?*

My Temptation Inventory

2. *Circle the number that best reflects your Temptation Tactics:*
   ❶ Strongly disagree. ❷ Slightly disagree. ❸ Unsure. ❹ Agree.
   ❺ Strongly agree.

____ Temptations and spiritual opposition aren't really a factor in my Christian life.

____ When I'm tempted, instead of running away, I plow ahead, trying to be strong.

____ Because I've been experiencing the joys of Jabez, I expect fewer temptations.

____ When I'm severely tempted, I assume God is testing me to make me strong.

____ Now that I experience God's hand, God will protect me from all temptations.

If Satan decided to custom-make a temptation to stop you dead in your tracks, what would it be?

____ YOUR SCORE: Total the values assigned to the five statements. If you scored…

> 21–25 *You can expect to overcome sin with God's help.*
> 16–20 *You can expect to overcome temptation.*
> 11–15 *You can expect to take a beating often.*
> 5–10 *You're taking a real beating…and you don't even know it.*

2. WHAT IS TEMPTATION, AND HOW DOES IT WORK?

KEY🔑   Temptation can be described as the pull we all feel to please ourselves at the expense of pleasing God. Think of temptation as a three-front war that all believers must face until they reach heaven's gate: temptations from the world, from our own wrong desires, and from the devil.

THE WORLD refers to the non-Christian values promoted by secular or pagan belief systems.

1.   *Read 1 John 2: 15—16. List the three elements of "the world" that tempt us. Describe how these temptations look where you live.*

2.   *What are the primary "world" temptations that your friends face on a regular basis? Which seem hardest to handle for most of them?*

3.   *Romans 12:2 says not to be "conformed to [poured into the mold of] this world, but be transformed by the renewing of your mind." When you look back on the world from eternity's point of view, how will you think differently about the world and its values?*

THE FLESH is the Bible's term for the sinful appetites that originate in our sin nature and physical desires. Even after salvation, these desires make us vulnerable to temptation.

1. *Read Galatians 5:16–21. List below the "works of the flesh" that Paul describes.*

2. *Have you seen flesh and Spirit at war in your life this past week (Galatians 5:17)? Explain.*

3. *When we begin to let the Lord work through us, our flesh takes notice. List a couple of the main temptations you might expect to face as God uses you more. How will you handle them?*

THE DEVIL is the tempter. Besides putting temptations in our path, Satan fiercely opposes God's will and work in us. Peter warns Christians that "your adversary the devil walks about like a roaring lion, seeking whom he may devour" (1 Peter 5:8).

1. *What does "roaring lion" help you understand about Satan's motives and methods? Why might he attack with more vengeance the people faithfully praying the Jabez prayer?*

2. *Read Ephesians 6:10–18 and list the primary pieces of armor used against the "schemes of the devil." Which ones do you feel you use successfully? Which do you need to understand and apply more?*

3. *Read Ephesians 6:12. Describe what you have to "wrestle" with as the enemy opposes your ministry in the home, church, and marketplace.*

3. WHAT BIBLE STORIES SHOW ME HOW TO AVOID TEMPTATION?

CASE STUDY #1
Joseph: young man, big future, target of temptation

[Read Genesis 39; 41:37—45]

KEY Joseph's story continues the chronicle of God's promised blessing to Abraham and his descendants (Joseph was Abraham's great-grandson). Joseph's older brothers resented him for being his father's favorite. Presented with an opportunity, they sold him into slavery in Egypt (37:18—36). Joseph quickly gained favor only to be betrayed again—this time by his master's wife.

1. *In Joseph's story, we see a remarkable example of how our experiences often follow the sequence of the four parts of the prayer of Jabez. Describe the evidence you find in each of the four areas:*

   a. Blessings (39:3, 5, 21, 23)

   b. Territory (39:2, 3, 5, 21, 23; 41:40—45)

   c. Power (39:3—6, 21—23; 41:38—40)

   d. Protection (39:7—12)

2. *Do you think Joseph was tempted by the world, the flesh, or the devil—or all three? Explain.*

3. *What steps could you take in your life to avoid major temptation? (For insights see 39:8, 10, 12.)*

CASE STUDY #2
Samson: strong man, big future, fool for temptation
[Read Judges 16]

eXTRA Israel's most famous strongman, Samson, may have lived during or near the same time as Jabez. Yet their stories could hardly be more different. Even before Samson was born, God promised his parents that their son would be special, set apart for God from birth to take territory for God—"and he shall begin to deliver Israel out of the hand of the Philistines" (Judges 13:5). But after a twenty-year career, Samson fell to temptation and not only experienced pain, but also brought great pain to the nation he was to deliver. What a negative illustration of the last part of the prayer of Jabez!

1. *Samson started his downfall by repeating the same sin twice (Judges 16:1, 4). Why does adultery bring with it so many other sins and temptations?*

2. *Judges 16:5 reveals Delilah's motive for destroying the man who loved her. How does the love of money tempt us to compromise? Read 1 Timothy 6:9–10 and list the consequences of the love of money. Have you seen this happen in real life?*

3. *When a person commits a major sin, it greatly affects others in its wake (see 2 Samuel 12:9–12). Share a time when someone else's sin greatly affected you. If you chose to follow in the footsteps of Samson, who would experience traumatic pain?*

4. SO HOW DO I WIN AGAINST TEMPTATION?

KEY This last part of Jabez's prayer, "that you would keep me from evil, that I may not cause pain!" mirrors the world's most famous prayer, known today as the Lord's Prayer. Jesus taught us to pray, "And do not lead us in temptation, but deliver us from the evil one."

1. *The Lord is active in protecting you when you are tempted, even before you ask. Read 1 Corinthians 10:13 for two important truths about temptations. How does that make you feel about how hard your temptations really are?*

   a. *God will not allow me to be tempted beyond what I am* _____.

   b. *God will make the way of escape so I can* _____.

2. *Read James 1:13–15. According to these verses, where does temptation not come from? What is the source of temptation?*

PRAYING KEEP AWAY

Think for a minute about how you pray when you face temptations. Do you mostly ask just for strength to not give in? There's nothing wrong with that prayer, but it's not the way Jabez prayed. He didn't pray "Keep me through evil" but "Keep me from evil." Jabez understood that our most important strategy for defeating the roaring lion is to stay out of the arena.

FROM *THE PRAYER OF JABEZ FOR TEENS*

3. *Write out the steps of progression between temptation and the ultimate consequence of giving in to temptation (James 1:14—15).*

4. HOW TO DEFEAT TEMPTATIONS FROM THE DEVIL.
    Do you know what advice the Bible gives for those times you face a "devil temptation"? Read James 4:7 and Ephesians 6:10—20 and describe three things you could do to assure victory.

5. HOW TO DEFEAT TEMPTATIONS FROM THE FLESH. *Read Galatians 5:16—18, 24—25 and Romans 8:5 and list the specific actions you should take to overcome a "flesh temptation."*

6. HOW TO DEFEAT TEMPTATIONS FROM THE WORLD. *Read James 4:4, 1 John 2:15, and Romans 12:2, then describe what the Bible presents as the answer when you face "world temptations."*

Even though Jesus taught that we should ask God to lead us away from temptation, why do you think most people rarely pray this way except in church?

5. HOW COULD MY LIFE CHANGE IF I ASKED GOD TO KEEP ME FROM EVIL?

eXTRA Browse through these *Prayer of Jabez* letters from www.prayerofjabez.com to see what others are learning about:

♦ how God wants us to pray, and how He answers.
♦ how we should respond during a temptation.
♦ how we will feel when we see God answer.

DANIEL DIDN'T QUIT

When I read that Daniel prayed for twenty-one days but the answer was hindered by Satan, the Lord showed me that I pray and then quit, pray and quit again. So I made a list of nine burdens and committed to pray for God's will in them each day. I have done so for fifty-three days now, and God has changed my heart. He has drawn a hedge around my family and on two occasions protected our home from fire. To God be the glory! There's nothing magical about praying certain things a certain number of times, but God honors our commitment.

SPIRIT CHECK

Praying to be kept from evil is already impacting my life. I have struggled with the same sin for years, and today at work it hit me again. But the Holy Spirit immediately checked my spirit, and I was able to flee from the temptation and resist the enemy.

A JABEZ HIDING IN NEHEMIAH

To my amazement, I found the Jabez prayer "concealed" in the text of Nehemiah 2:4—9—not only the structure of the prayer, but even the same sequence. Talk about confirmation! I saw the pattern of blessing (Nehemiah was granted his request), enlarging the territories (he was given timber for construction), and the hand of God upon him (actually stated in verse 8). I thought "keep me from evil" wasn't there until I got to the next paragraph: "The king, I should add, had sent along army officers and horsemen to protect me" (Nehemiah 2:9, NLT). Astounding!

Taste Test

Last night while driving to work, I prayed that God would deliver me from temptation. When I arrived at work, a group home for adolescents, I found that the policy had been changed to allow only family-rated movies. Also, the teens can no longer hang posters or pictures that are in bad taste. As I said to my coworker— "Praise the Lord!"

"That I Would Not Cause Pain"

I wish I had been praying this prayer for the last thirty years. I have always been preoccupied with being right, with having the best argument. As I began to pray, God convicted me of the severe insensitivity I've shown to those I love. He showed me times when I hurt my children and my wife with angry, demeaning words and attitudes. Each time I tried to pray the prayer of Jabez, God would bring similar memories to mind as if to say, "Do you mean this, 'that I would not cause pain'?" My heart broke as I felt the pain I've thoughtlessly inflicted on others, and I have pledged that I will do all I can to make things right. God has given me opportunities to admit that I have been cruel and to ask forgiveness. It's been hard because I have littered my past with rash statements and actions, often in the name of God. But I'm thankful that today He is blessing me indeed. There is territory in the hearts of my children and my wife that He is granting back to me in miraculous ways.

Sin Is a Big Pain

Linked to Jabez's last request are the words "that I may not cause pain." Many translations render the clause "so that I will be free from pain" or something similar. The Hebrew simply says "pain not," so you can see why both renderings can be correct...and completely true.

Sin causes pain, period. The Bible says, "The wages of sin is death" (Romans 6:23). Satan wants you to sin because he wants to cut you off not only from God's blessings but also from your relationship with Him. Why? Because Satan wants to hurt you!

FROM *The Prayer of Jabez for Teens*

6. WHAT KEEPS ME FROM ENJOYING GOD'S PROTECTION?

KEY Do you recognize old attitudes and habits about temptation that are leaving you exposed? Check yes or no to the following questions:

SNAKE-EYED THOUGHTS & TOXIC FUMES

☐ Yes ☐ No 1. "AUTO" INSURED. *"I think that if I'm a Christian and live right, I'll automatically be covered against evil attacks."*

☐ Yes ☐ No 2. UNDERPOWERED & OVERWHELMED. *"You don't know how intense my temptations are! I just can't handle them; they overpower me."*

☐ Yes ☐ No 3. TEMPTATION JUNKIE. *"Why flee my temptations? I can survive, and I like the thrill of 'standing on the edge.'"*

☐ Yes ☐ No 4. DEVIL DOUBTER. *"I don't really believe all that occult stuff about Satan and spiritual opposition."*

☐ Yes ☐ No 5. CHOOSE TO LOSE. *"Why start over when you know you'll fail again? I think some sins are just meant to be part of us, like a mole or a scar."*

☐ Yes ☐ No 6. HOME ALONE. *"I'm not sure I trust God to be there when I need Him. Anyway, when I'm being tempted I don't feel worthy of God's help."*

Now read the truth in the references below, then paraphrase the truth as a new breakthrough belief for your life.

SNAKE REPELLENT & POISON CONTROL

1. "AUTO" INSURED? Read Galatians 6:1; 2 Peter 2:9; Matthew 26:41; 1 John 1:8–10.
   The truth is...

2. UNDERPOWERED & OVERWHELMED? Read 1 Corinthians 10:13; Hebrews 12:3–4; Hebrews 4:15–16.
   The truth is...

3. TEMPTATION JUNKIE? Read 1 Corinthians 9:24–10:12; Proverbs 6:27–28.
   The truth is...

4. DEVIL DOUBTER? Read Matthew 4:1–11; 1 Peter 5:18; Ephesians 6:10–18.
   The truth is...

5. CHOOSE TO LOSE? Read Romans 6:11–13, 15; 8:1–5; James 1:12–17; 1 John 4:4.
   The truth is...

6. HOME ALONE? Read James 1:13–14; Hebrews 2:14–18; 4:14–16; 2 Peter 2:9.
   The truth is...

MY NEW START IN EXPERIENCING GOD'S PROTECTION FROM EVIL

To close this study on God's protection from evil, pray the following prayer aloud together. Then pray it on your own every day in the coming week.

My Prayer for Protection

Dear Lord,
Thank You for the priceless gift
of knowing and serving the Lord Jesus.
Forgive me for my frivolous attitude about sin
and my insensitivity to the things that grieve Your heart.
How deeply I desire to live a life of holiness
and to please You in every way.
Today I echo the words of Jesus when I plead,
"Lead me not into temptation, but deliver me from evil."
Please, Lord, keep me from evil,
that I may not cause pain to You, or others, or myself.
Instead, may I bring delight to You
and may Your will be done on earth
as it is in heaven, beginning here with me.
Amen

Now to Him who is able to keep you from stumbling, and to present you faultless before the presence of His glory with exceeding joy, to God our Savior, who alone is wise, be glory and majesty, dominion and power, both now and forever. Amen.

JUDE 1:24–25

Maximize Your Impact for God

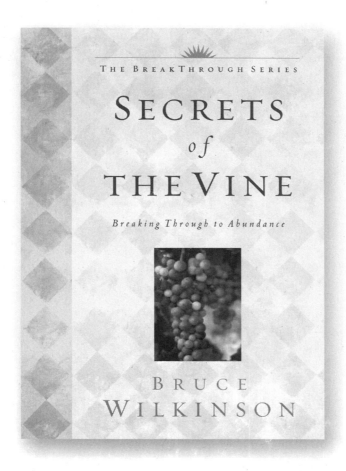

Dr. Bruce Wilkinson explores John 15 to show readers how to make maximum impact for God. Dr. Wilkinson demonstrates how Jesus is the Vine of life, discusses four levels of "fruit bearing" (doing the good work of God), and reveals three life-changing truths that will lead readers to new joy and effectiveness in His kingdom.

ISBN 1-57673-975-9

Also available on audiocassette, ISBN 1-57673-977-5

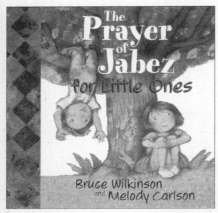